IMAGES
of America

OLD VERONA

Bloomfield Avenue, Verona, N. J.

This is Verona center (east of Grove Avenue) as it appeared about 1905.

IMAGES
of America

OLD VERONA

Robert L. Williams

ARCADIA

First published 1998
Copyright © Robert L. Williams, 1998

ISBN 0-7524-0992-1

Published by Arcadia Publishing,
an imprint of the Chalford Publishing Corporation,
One Washington Center, Dover, New Hampshire 03820.
Printed in Great Britain

Library of Congress Cataloging-in-Publication Data applied for

Contents

Acknowledgments

The author wishes to express his sincere appreciation to Dr. Dewitt C. Baldwin, Dorothy Budd Bartle, Laura Staedler Beck, Archer Bush, Marguerite Wilder Carrington, Gene Collerd, Kathryn Corwin, Jonathan P. Glasby III, Alice Ryan, Ann Watkins, Robert J. Williams, and Walter P. Williams for the use of their irreplaceable old photographs. Both the Verona and Newark Public Libraries as well as the Verona Methodist Church also allowed the use of their photographic material and thus helped to further this endeavor. Noted artist Robert Lahm painstakingly prepared three beautiful paintings of early buildings which would not have been included if it weren't for his able assistance. A sincere thank you goes to David Brooks, Robert Bush, and Alleine Graef, who edited the manuscript, and to New Jersey's foremost historian, John T. Cunningham, for his advice and guidance in the beginning stages. My wife, Bonnie Williams, faithfully delivered all the photographs to Krauss Photo Service in Port Jervis, New York, where they were carefully and professionally handled. Last but not least, a debt of gratitude is owed to the many people who graciously shared their memories of Verona's former days. Without their undying support and encouragement, this book would not have been possible. It is to all of the above that *Old Verona* is dedicated.

Introduction

Nestled between the gentle folds of the First and Second Watchung Mountains of western Essex County lies Verona Township. It is a valley town divided by the Peckman River, which flows northward from West Orange to Little Falls, where it joins the Passaic River. Today Verona is thriving and, like its surrounding communities, it is busy with the hustle and bustle of modern-day activity. While probably unknown to many, our community is one with a proud and shining heritage.

Settled early in the 18th century by pioneers who moved northwest from Newark or southwest from the Paterson area, the Verona scene was dominated for many decades by small farmsteads that had been carved into the virgin wilderness. Like its counterparts, Verona had its mills, blacksmith shops, and general stores, which supported the agricultural base. Many labored long and hard, and from all accounts, life was rigorous. By the turn of the 19th century only a handful of families had settled in the area, but vast changes were about to take place.

In 1806 work began on the Newark and Pompton Turnpike—what is today known as Bloomfield and Pompton Avenues. A vast improvement from the earlier pioneer roads, which had the tendency to meander and were poorly maintained, the new road allowed local residents to travel more easily to the markets of Newark and Paterson. Not long after the Civil War, another attempt was made to improve travel when a rail line was proposed that would parallel Bloomfield Avenue. Work was begun on a tunnel through the First Mountain and embankments were created through the valley. The project lured speculators like Captain Hiram Cook, and though the rail line met with failure, Cook and others remained. Cook's vision and foresight were ultimately responsible for transforming an unimproved mill pond into Verona Lake, which became a Mecca for those seeking recreation.

The 1890s were a boom time for Verona. Early in the decade a railroad line was constructed through the northern portion of the community, and by the end of the decade residents could enjoy uninterrupted trolley service to Newark. With the improved transportation came new families who would make Verona their home and slowly transform it from an agricultural community into a bedroom suburb of Newark and New York. By the turn of the century the population had swelled to more than 800.

As Verona grew, its residents developed new needs. Since 1798 Verona (or Vernon as it was once called) had been a part of old Caldwell Township, which was comprised of about half a dozen communities.* In the closing years of the 19th century many local residents felt their tax dollars were going to work in other areas of the township, so in 1892 both Verona and Cedar Grove separated from the old township and created Verona Township. This union would not be long lived because the development of Verona exceeded that of Cedar Grove. In 1907 Verona residents wanted an up-to-date water system, but this was considered an extravagance to Cedar Grove. The two communities amicably parted company and the Borough of Verona was created.

Many communities recognize their past through their remaining historic landmarks. Although Verona has lost many of its early and most fascinating sites, some survive and firmly stand their ground as silent testimonials to a proud but almost forgotten era. Behind every house is the story of the people who lived in it. Many of these people made significant contributions in molding our community and some paid the ultimate price while defending the liberties and freedom of our nation. Some of their stories have been included.

This book is not meant to be an in-depth history, but an attempt to open the door to Verona's early days through the use of historic pictures. Some of these images were found in local attics and graciously lent for this endeavor, while others were rescued over the years from trash piles. Each is a picture-perfect image of where we have been and perhaps provides an understanding of where we are today. As you turn the page, prepare to embark on a journey through Old Verona.

*Note: Prior to the establishment of Caldwell Township, the West Essex region was known as the Horseneck Tract, which had been purchased from Native Americans in 1702 by the town fathers of Newark.

One
Working to Survive

Local tradition holds that Verona was first settled by Mr. Butters around 1730. His primitive farmstead was located in the southeastern section of Verona and for many years Sunset Avenue was called Butterstown Road. From the early days to the closing decades of the 19th century the makeup of Verona was dominated by small farms. The exact location of this photograph is unknown, but it is believed to have been taken in Verona about 1898.

Some farms included their own orchards where peaches and apples were grown for the family and, if fortune permitted, for sale. This venerable old orchard was located on Dewitt C. Baldwin's farm on Sunset Avenue. The property had been in the Baldwin family since the 18th century. This photo was taken about 1893.

The sight of a hay wagon passing by was not uncommon in the last century. Al Harris (right), with his cousins Marjorie and Will, are posed in front of a wagon on Claremont Avenue between Elmwood and Westview Roads in the mid-1890s. Claremont Avenue as a thoroughfare dates back to pioneer days. Local settlers depended upon this road for the transportation of their goods to the markets in Newark.

Many people pass over the Peckman River without thinking of the role it played in Verona's development. It is believed to have taken its name from a Native American word which translates to cranberry, and it is speculated that cranberries once grew wild along its banks. In Verona's early days the Peckman provided waterpower for two mills. This photo was taken about 1900 probably north of the Bloomfield Avenue bridge.

In 1794 Christian Bone, Verona's first doctor, purchased nearly 4 acres on the south corner of what is today Lakeside and Bloomfield Avenues. Local history records that 20 years later he built the first dam and gristmill. When this photo was taken in the mid-1890s, Verona Lake had seen little change from its days as a mill pond.

The gristmill stood along the south side of Bloomfield Avenue adjacent to the present-day bridge and served as a local landmark for many years. The only remains of this endeavor are several ledgers and a copper stencil plate which date to the Ettenborough ownership. An old millstone also survives. Thomas Ettenborough, an English immigrant, purchased the mill in the early 1830s from Joseph and Moses Jacobus. The mill passed through several other hands before it was removed in the late 1890s. A July 30, 1898 *Caldwell News* article records, "The old Dr. Bone mill that was recently sold at auction will soon be a thing of the past. The terms upon which the mill and its contents were sold called for its removal before January 1, 1899. It is presumed before another year dawns, that its removal will be accomplished, and the unsightly structure that has been the rendezvous for tramps and people of questionable character, will be torn down, and the appearance of the village considerably improved." This painting shows the mill as it appeared in its final days.

Verona's first recorded gristmill was established in 1790 and located near the Cedar Grove border. In 1831 it was purchased by Nicholas Stagg and Cornelius Jacobus, who enlarged the business by providing machinery for sawing and turning. Until recently the only vestige to survive of this early operation was the old Stagg residence, which dated to the 1860s. This rear view photo was taken about 1925.

The Stagg Homestead was elegant for its day and attested to the prosperity of the Stagg operation. When demolished in 1997, it was discovered that the pegs used to pin the frame together had been turned, and it is speculated that these were made in the mill. Prior to the construction of this home, an earlier dwelling stood on the site. This photo was taken about 1925 when the house served as the residence of August Ahlborn.

Located in the basement of the Stagg Homestead was a brick beehive bake oven used in the baking of breads and cakes. This antiquated feature was quite unusual for a house of this late period. Perhaps Rebecca Stagg was used to such an oven in the earlier dwelling and demanded this in the new house. The oven was removed brick by brick before the house was demolished.

Time seemed to have stood still in the attic of the Stagg Homestead. A recent owner recalled locating Civil War documents and a belt buckle between the floor joists. These originally belonged to William Grosch, who resided here with his family from 1876 until his death 20 years later. The relics have unfortunately disappeared. Concealed on the upper window sash was written, "Charles R. Lyons, Painter & Paper Hanger, Montclair, N.J. 1897."

Henry Ahlborn and his partner, William Grosch, purchased the Stagg mill in 1876, where they relocated their bronze powder manufacturing business. Their venture was founded in Brooklyn in 1873 but quickly outgrew the original factory. Grosch and, initially, Ahlborn, made the Stagg Homestead their home. This photo of Ahlborn and his wife, Clara Backus, was taken about 1930.

The manufacturing of bronze powder was a profitable venture, and, until 1903, this was the only company of its kind in the western hemisphere. Its product was used in wallpaper decorating (some examples remained in the old house), labels, paint, art work, and the finest grade reserved for printing ink. This view was taken from the site of the present-day sewage plant about 1918.

As business at the Bronze Mill grew, Henry Ahlborn had this Queen Anne-style Victorian mansion constructed in the early 1890s, and to this day it remains one of the largest homes in Verona. It stands on the north corner of Fairview Avenue and Personette Street. Ahlborn's property stretched from Fairview Avenue to the crest of the Second Mountain.

Henry and August Ahlborn pose with the millworkers for this 1918 photo. Former employees recall how the bronze powder covered everything in the mill, clinging to the worker's clothing as well as the machinery.

During the early years work at the American Bronze Powder Manufacturing Company was kept secret, as Grosch and Ahlborn were apprehensive of European agents who desired to learn their manufacturing process. The mill generated a great deal of noise due to the large stamp mills which pulverized the bronze strips into powder. When the western corner of the mill complex was demolished in 1997, powder was discovered under the sill plates.

Two millworkers pose inside the mill in the 1930s. In 1939, after Ahlborn's death, the American Bronze Powder Company became a subsidiary of Metals Disintegrating of Elizabeth. It is noted that the company played a minor role in the Manhattan Project of World War II and pulverized magnesium for the war effort.

Verona's first general store was established by John and Caleb Baldwin along the north side of Bloomfield Avenue in 1834. It operated without competition until mid-century when Alex Gould opened a store nearby. The Baldwin store passed through several hands before it was destroyed by fire in 1867. It was rebuilt by William L. Scott that same year and in 1881 was purchased by Charles S. Simonson. This photo showing the attached post office was taken in the 1890s. Research reveals that the post office was located at this site since its founding in 1857. For many years prior to this date Verona was known as Vernon. When application was made for the establishment of a post office under this name, it was learned that there was already a Vernon (in Sussex County), so local residents chose the name of Verona.

Methodist Church & Post Office, Verona N. J.

The Simonson store was replaced with this up-to-date brick building in 1909. Two bluestones embedded in the upper portion of the front facade read, "Simonson 1909." The old Methodist church stood on the corner of Grove and Bloomfield Avenue adjacent to the store.

In the 1920s Verona residents would go to this building to collect their mail. Today it serves as the Janett Real Estate office and is located on the east corner of Bloomfield Avenue and Park Place. The post office would later be removed to a brick building on Montrose Avenue to the rear of Dipaolo's Bakery.

Many older residents remember the blacksmith shop which stood on the south side of Bloomfield Avenue where the Pancake House is now located. It was built in 1881 and replaced an older shop that had been destroyed by fire in the summer of 1880. The occupations of smithy and wheelwright were combined in this brick building, and there were facilities on the second floor for carriage making and painting.

In 1893 W.P. Johnson erected a three-story building, where he established a grocery and feed store. He rented the west side of the store to his cousin, W.P. Rich, who operated the Verona Pharmacy. In 1899 Judge Johnson built the adjacent building and Rich moved to that location. Both buildings remain. To the far left is the Walker residence, which still stands; to the right is the Dobbins Homestead, which was demolished in 1985.

It was not uncommon to see W.P. Johnson or his assistant traveling the countryside in a grocery wagon, from which they would take orders and deliver goods. When horseless carriages were becoming popular, one traveling on Sunset Avenue frightened Johnson's horse, which resulted in the overturning of the wagon.

Lemuel Jacobus settled in Verona around 1830 and five years later established his brush factory. The company manufactured scrubbing brushes, horse brushes, and paint brushes. Traveling salesmen loaded their wagons and peddled the company goods throughout the area. The business operated at several locations before moving to this site opposite present-day Forest Avenue in 1908. The brush factory has long passed into history, but the old building still survives.

John Williams had this modest house and attached grocery store constructed on Claremont Avenue opposite Malvern about 1890. He was frequently seen traveling the local area in his grocery wagon taking orders and delivering goods. He died in 1894 at the young age of 42, and his son Walter took over the business until it was discontinued a few years later. The house still stands but has undergone much change.

Many old-timers remember Schmid's Hardware, which stood on Bloomfield Avenue opposite Church Street. Ed Schmid, referred to by many as "Hardware Schmid," built this Victorian-era store about 1894. Schmid stocked everything from tools and kerosene lamps to china. This photo was taken in the late 1930s.

This close-up of the front of Schmid's Hardware shows the old hitching post where horses were tethered while patrons shopped inside. When the store and adjoining house were demolished in 1948, this relic was removed and remains preserved in Verona.

West of the store was located Schmid's residence. This elegant Victorian building was probably built in the 1880s. The photograph was taken just before its demolition. Many antique bottles such as Dr. Kilmer's Swamp Root Kidney Cure and Peterman's Bed Bug Cure were found buried in the bank a short distance behind the house.

In the days when stores were few, local businesses made deliveries directly to their patrons' homes. The milkman pictured above may have just delivered to Fillmore Condit's newly built home shown in the background. The Condit residence was located on the corner of Elmwood Road and Bloomfield Avenue—it still stands behind the gas station which was constructed on the front lawn. This view dates from the 1890s.

Harry Parkhurst operated a well-drilling business from his home on Bloomfield Avenue, where the modern office building occupied by the Red Cross is now located. Parkhurst is standing beside his two associates in this photo from about 1914.

J. Edgar Williams's remnant business, established on Claremont Avenue at the head of Church Street in 1878, proved to be a successful operation, drawing a patronage from far and wide. He contracted with the textile mills in Paterson and Passaic for their ends and seconds, which he sold at his store. Patrons could purchase small pieces as well as yards of cloth, which would then be used in the making of quilts and clothes.

As Verona grew, its increased population provided the opportunity for more businesses such as Petrulio Brothers Barber Shop. Alfred Petrulio, an Italian immigrant, was about 15 years old when this photo was taken in 1906. He and his two brothers, Frank and Leo, ran the shop. The old building still stands and can be found on Bloomfield Avenue adjacent to the Verona Post Office.

At the turn of the 20th century, urban dwellers migrated to western Essex County to vacation in one of the several large hotels in that vicinity. One was the Hotel Montclair, which stood high atop the First Mountain on the Montclair/Verona border. The exterior of the building was stuccoed exclusively in Dexter Portland Cement. Pompton Avenue is barely noticeable in the foreground.

The site of the Montclair commanded an excellent view of points east and west. Rooms could be had for a day, week, or month, and the hotel was equipped with a grill and tap room. The landmark was removed years ago and replaced with the present Rockcliff Apartments. During the days of the Revolutionary War, Washington's troops would use this vantage point to survey the movement of the British in New York.

As Verona progressed into the 20th century, new businesses were created and new store buildings constructed. This store building, located on the west corner of Lakeside and Bloomfield Avenues, still survives. Erected in the 1920s, the vintage of the postcard, it then housed White's Market. The corner was originally the site of William G. Jacobus's general store, which is known to have operated in the 1870s.

Two

Touring the Center

In the 1830s Verona center was comprised of a handful of buildings, including a church, schoolhouse, and one general store. Expansion would be slow but by the late 1850s, buildings would dot both sides of Bloomfield Avenue from Lakeside to Grove Avenue and beyond. Among them could be found a drugstore, two general stores, a blacksmith shop, and a brush factory. Walling's 1859 map of Essex County shows that important local families such as the Goulds, Personetts, Dobbins's, and Jacobus's were well established in the community.

Development continued to be gradual, and by 1910 Verona center included a modest number of businesses along with the Firehouse/Borough Hall, which stood on the corner of Grove and Bloomfield Avenues in the former Methodist church. The brick building to the right is the Simonson store, which still stands today. Next to Simonson's, at the far right of the photo, is Adam Wiessmann's butcher shop, which is now occupied by an upholstering business. Mr. Wiessmann tragically lost his life when he courageously stepped out into Bloomfield Avenue to stop a team of runaway horses that posed a threat to children at the nearby Bloomfield Avenue School.

Bloomfield Ave., East of Fairview Ave., Verona, N. J.

Bloomfield Avenue was once a peaceful and quaint thoroughfare free of rush-hour congestion. This *c.* 1910 postcard view was taken east of Fairview Avenue. The small house facing the road was the Jacobus home, which may have been built in the mid-19th century. The white building to the left was the former Dobbins Homestead. Both landmarks have passed into history.

Few buildings seen in this *c.* 1908 postcard of the center survive. The old Methodist church standing to the left was soon to become the firehouse/town hall. To the right is a small building which served as the Verona Post Office. This building was moved and today stands on the north side of Linden Avenue east of Grove. Next to the post office is Wiessmann's butcher shop, which still stands.

Grove Avenue dates back to the pioneer days and was initially known as Gould Lane. As today, this thoroughfare connected Verona center with Cedar Grove center. The building to the left is Johnson's store and to the right is Verona's Firehouse/Borough Hall. This postcard view dates to 1911.

By 1920 the appearance of Grove Avenue had changed little. This view was taken about a half mile north of the center. Many of Verona's finest farms were located along this road. As the borough grew, the land along the southern portion of the road developed first. The Jacobus farm was Verona's last operating farmstead and was located on the west side of Grove Avenue a short distance north of Durrell Street.

At the end of the 19th century, rail transportation, train and trolley, enabled many city dwellers to move to the country. South Prospect Street, nearly opposite Grove Avenue, was built through the Dobbins farm, and property on each side was subdivided into building lots that were made available for purchase in the early 1890s.

Veronans have always loved a good parade. This 1918 photo shows the Home Guard marching down Bloomfield Avenue east of the present civic center. The function of the Home Guard was to protect the townspeople while the regulars were overseas engaged in combat. Notice the old trolley tracks and the Belgium Block between them. These are today buried under layers of tar.

Bloomfield Avenue was an open road with little traffic at the turn of the century. Lakeside Avenue is to the left along with the entrance to Verona Lake, and the small house in between once served as the miller's residence (the old mill stood adjacent to the bridge). The white building to the right was Max Liesenberg's Verona Hotel. Built in the 1890s, the old building still stands nearly opposite Lakeside Avenue.

Like many of Verona's roads years ago, Lakeside Avenue was a narrow thoroughfare when this 1920s postcard view was taken. Few know that Lakeside was once considered one of the most fashionable places to live in Verona. Large and prestigious homes such as those owned by the Mau, Cimiotti, Hornfeck, and Pease families were built on the hillside overlooking Verona Lake in the Victorian era.

VERONA CIVIC CENTER,
VERONA, N.J.

Verona's civic center was built in 1923 and ever since has been the heart of the community. It was once considered one of the finest in the nation and was the envy of all surrounding towns. It replaced the old Dr. Bone Homestead and two frame buildings on Bloomfield Avenue which originally served as schoolhouses (at different times). Several buildings on Gould Street were moved to Grove Avenue. As the borough grew, so did the civic center. Wings were added later to both the school and the library.

A February 1923 *Caldwell Progress* news article noted that the new municipal building was estimated to cost $75,000, a far cry from the cost of the new community center. Hector Hamilton of New York was selected by the council as the architect. His plans were chosen by the building committee as the best of ten entered in a competition.

The Verona Public Library opened the doors of its present building on September 7, 1923, but traces its history to 1893, when Anna DeGolier established the Isabella Literary Club—the forerunner of the Verona Women's Club. At one of their first meetings, DeGolier's group established a club library. Seven years later, following a joint meeting with a citizens' committee in February 1900, the Verona Public Library Association was formed and the club's books were turned over to the association. The library was housed in several locations before moving to the former Firehouse/Borough Hall, where most of its books were destroyed by fire in January 1923. This view dates to 1923.

A drive to raise $5,500 was inaugurated in March 1924 to erect this war memorial in the heart of the civic center. During a meeting Mayor David Slayback told the audience of the days when the boys were leaving for the front and how they were promised that when they returned, Verona would perpetuate their memory in a fitting memorial. He continued by saying that, once erected, the monument would be a partial payment for a debt which the town could never fully repay. The statue was unveiled in June 1924 before a crowd of several hundred people. During the dedication, J.M. Harris, in his speech, noted that Verona had sent 135 men off to war, three of whom died in the line of duty. After the band played the "Star Spangled Banner," Irving Conway, commander of Wittenweiler Post, gave the command to unveil the memorial. This photo was taken immediately after the unveiling.

Three
Where We Gathered

High atop the Second Mountain is located the White Rock, which, according to local tradition, was one of the first religious gathering places in the community. No written documentation has yet been discovered to verify this, but it was not uncommon years ago to have an outdoor worship service as a special evangelistic event to convert non-believers. This postcard view dates to about 1918.

For many years the land around and below the rock was cleared, thus providing an excellent view of the Verona Valley. This photo was taken by Jon Glasby while home on furlough in 1944. Today, the landmark boulder sits in obscurity shrouded by trees that protect it from the modern sights and sounds in the valley below. In its present state it is one of Verona's prettiest and most serene sites.

The Methodists were the first religious congregation to organize in Verona. Their initial house of worship was built on the corner of Bloomfield and Grove Avenues in 1833. It was a plain building nearly square in shape with clear glass windows. The interior, containing a gallery and the pulpit platform against the rear wall, was flanked by a set of steps. In 1873 the building was extensively remodeled and enlarged by local contractor Hiram Cook. The renovations included decorative stained-glass windows and two towers, one of which contained a bell. The interior ceiling was painted to resemble the sky, complete with stars and clouds. The remodeling cost $6,450—over five times the amount of the cost to build the original building. This photo dates to about 1890.

TEMPERANCE
MASS MEETING
AND
STRAWBERRY FESTIVAL!
For the Benefit of the
M. E. CHURCH AT VERNON,
To be held in the Grove of Mr. JOSEPH PERSONETT, on
THURSDAY, JUNE 19
ADDRESSES AT 10 A. M. and 3 P. M. By

Rev. I. W. WILEY, late Missionary to China.

Rev. M. E. ELLISON, of Newark.

Rev. S. L. TUTTLE, of Madison.

Rev. J. SCARLETT, of Bloomfield.

Rev. J. M. FREEMAN, of Orange.

☛ A BRASS BAND will be in attendance
THROUGHOUT THE DAY.

☛ DINNER, SUPPER and other REFRESHMENTS provided on the Ground. ☚

☛ COME ONE, COME ALL ! ☚
☛ Should the weather prove unfavorable, the Meeting will take place on the next fair day.

VERNON, June 2d 1858.

ISAAC J. OLIVER'S United States Steam Printing Establishment, 32 Beekman-Street, New-York.

The congregation maintains a large collection of documents detailing the early history of the church and the vital role it played in the early years of the community. This temperance poster dates to 1856 when Verona was known as Vernon. The meeting was to be held in Personett's Grove, which was located behind the Personett Homestead on the west side of Grove Avenue.

In 1909 the Methodists built their present edifice on Montrose Avenue, selling the original building to Verona. The old building was retrofitted to accommodate the police and fire departments and eventually the library. In the attached Sunday school building were the borough offices. In 1923, while the civic center was under construction, the original church was destroyed by fire. All that remained was the rear annex, which was moved to South Prospect Street where it stands today.

The Presbyterians were the second denomination to establish themselves in Verona and organized in 1894. Their first service was held on January 21 in Johnson's new hall on the corner of Grove and Bloomfield Avenues. Their first minister was Rev. Edward Lloyd. Eight years after their organization, the congregation had the financial wherewithal to build their first house of worship on the corner of Fairview Avenue and Pine Street.

The interior of the Presbyterian church was trimmed with gulf cypress, and the pews were made of oak. The sanctuary had a seating capacity of 350, and the backs of the pews were reversible so that Sunday school classes could be held there. The old church was replaced in 1953 with the present sanctuary. This view dates to 1940.

In 1930 the brick wing was added to the church complex and houses Chamberlain Hall, named in honor of Rev. Pierce Chamberlain, who served the church from 1909 to 1929. The wing still stands and appears much the way as shown in this c. 1935 postcard.

The Congregationalists were the last denomination to organize in Verona in the closing years of the 19th century. Their first service was held in March 1896 in the Verona Club House. The new church was finished the following year and was complete with electric lighting—a novelty for the time. The postcard view, c. 1906, shows the building as it originally appeared. In 1914 the church was expanded and remodeled.

In 1905 the Congregational Parsonage was built on Malvern Street behind the church. Its first occupants were Reverend Pratt and his family. It is said that when this house was built, fields of daisies and Queen Anne's Lace stretched out in all directions. This postcard view dates to 1907, and the old building still serves its original purpose.

Other denominations would establish themselves in Verona in the decades of the 20th century. Work began in erecting Our Lady of the Lake Roman Catholic Church on Lakeside Avenue in 1924, and the first Masses offered in the building took place on Ascension Day, May 24. Over 200 people were in attendance. The old building still stands but was replaced with a new church edifice in 1964.

Little is known about Verona's first schoolhouse, which is believed to date to about 1770. It was a log structure and its exact location is unknown. This schoolhouse was built in 1851 and occupied until the original portion of the brick Bloomfield Avenue School was built in 1881. Reportedly, the seats and desks were crudely assembled from planks, and a large stove occupied the center of the classroom.

Once the new brick Bloomfield Avenue School was built, the old building was sold for $505 and converted into a store. The building to the right was reportedly an earlier school. When the civic center was built in 1923, that house was moved and today is located at 206 Linden Avenue.

The original portion of the brick Bloomfield Avenue School was designed by Paul Botticher of Newark, and bids were awarded to Amzi Sigler for the masonry and Warren Taylor for the carpentry. The new school was completed and ready for occupancy the following year. This school photo taken about 1890 shows the former Dr. Bone house to the left.

Young students along with their two teachers are dressed in their best clothes for this 1890s photo. Before the old Bloomfield Avenue School was demolished, a couple of artifacts were found in the basement, including an old brass key, school books, and a bell that was almost obscured by layers of dust and dirt.

Desks in the new school contained fancy cast-iron supports, as shown in this photo of about 1895. To control sunlight in the rooms, tall shutters were installed on interior windows. Initially there was no indoor plumbing but instead two outhouses in the rear yard—one for boys and the other for girls.

In 1902–03 the school was expanded and remodeled to appear the way many remember it today. The new east addition contained six classrooms, a large hall, and floors of Georgia pine. When people talk of the old red school, this is the building to which they refer. The building was a true local landmark but would not survive to celebrate its 100th anniversary, as it was razed in 1970.

As Verona grew, additional classrooms were needed, so in 1911 a rear addition was made to the Bloomfield Avenue School. Twelve years later the original center portion of what was then the high school was constructed. The new building was dedicated in honor of local physician Henry B. Whitehorne in 1928.

The Mount Prospect Institute was another school associated with Verona. It was established as a private boarding school about 1838 by Warren Holt on the Montclair/Verona boundary, where the present-day Dorchester Apartments are located. This c. 1890 view shows the building as it appeared after an extensive remodeling in the Victorian era. At this time it served as a noted boardinghouse called the Mountain House.

An 1840s pamphlet about the institute noted that the governing of the school was conducted on strict religious principles and that the students were compelled to adhere to a uniform dress code. English, mathematics, drawing, painting, music, and selected foreign languages were among the subjects taught. The school proved to be an unprofitable venture and eventually was discontinued. This photo was taken a few years prior to the previous picture.

Above the stone outcropping beside the Mountain House was located this Victorian gazebo from which patrons enjoyed the spectacular view of points eastward. During the Revolutionary War, this ridge was used to survey the movements of the British troops. Today, the old gazebo has long disappeared, and this site is overgrown, but one can still make out each crack and crevice in the stones in this *c.* 1890 photo.

The Newark City Home was established in Verona in the early 1870s on property which is today the grounds of the Verona High School. The purpose of the home was to reform the children of Newark who "were treading the downward path" and for homeless orphans. The original portion of the main building was opened in 1874 on the hill facing Grove Avenue. Two years later a large north block with mansard roof and cupola with attaching hyphen was constructed. This engraving shows the building as it appeared after the north block and its attaching hyphen were built. It was a spectacular example of Victorian architecture and was once the largest building in the Verona Valley.

At the City Home the children, called "inmates," were not only educated but taught an occupation. The institution was self-sufficient with its own bakery, tailor shop, and farm. In December 1899, 189 boys and 26 girls were on the roll. The Assembly Room shown here was located in the 1892 wing of the main building.

Children on their best behavior are seated in the Primary Room of the City Home. Prior to 1901 a child, or inmate, was considered eligible for parole if he or she had earned ten badges of merit. Each inmate had the ability to earn ten merits daily—poor behavior was subject to demerits. This picture dates to the mid-1890s. Notice the old-fashioned desks and gas lamp fixtures.

A print shop was established at the City Home so that selected inmates could be taught the printing trade. Perhaps the most significant contribution of this department was the creation of *The Caldwell News*, which for many years was the only newspaper printed west of the First Mountain in Essex County. It was to serve as a teaching medium. The first issue was printed on February 4, 1892.

Like the other photos, this view dates to the mid-1890s and shows the new dormitory and obedient children posing by their beds. On the evening of January 9, 1900, this building was destroyed by fire. As a locomotive passed in the vicinity, the conductor sounded his whistle to warn the residents of the burning building. When discovered, the officials marched the children out of the home in perfect order. There were no casualties.

Soon after the destruction of the old building, a group of brick buildings referred to as cottages were constructed. Each was controlled by a master and matron, and it was felt that it was better to group the children in this family-like environment as opposed to the old system of mass congregation. This photo of the Administration Building dates to about 1902.

Children are seen playing behind the boys' cottages in this *c.* 1918 postcard. These buildings stand in the approximate location of the present-day high school. Like the old building, the cottages faced in the direction of Grove Avenue.

During World War I the occupants of the cottages were organized into military companies called the Newark City Home Cadet Corps. This 1918 photo shows the City Home boys in uniform marching down Bloomfield Avenue in the vicinity of present-day Terry's Drugs.

After the destruction of the old building in 1900, the girls were segregated from the boys in the cottage system. The Girls' Administration Building was erected on the crest of the Second Mountain northwest of the boys' cottages. Due to decreasing enrollment, the girls' school was phased out in 1906 and the building sat idle for a short period of time.

Through the efforts of two Montclair women, the abandoned girls' home became the Newark City Sanitarium for those suffering from tuberculosis in 1907. It is said that the mountain top was considered second only to Denver for beneficial results. This photo of patients was taken about 1912.

In 1917 the sanitarium was taken over by Essex County because T.B. had become a county problem. Shortly after, the County assumed control and construction began on 11 buildings, which were completed and open to patients in 1922. By 1935, the vintage of this postcard, additional buildings had been added to the sanitarium complex.

After the discovery of streptomycin and INH in the 1950s, the number of patients at the sanitarium began to slowly decline. Eventually the majority of the buildings were abandoned and became a playground for vandals. Windows were smashed, buildings were burned, and items of value were looted. This May 1993 photo was taken in the former auditorium located near the chapel.

The hallway on the top floor of what was once the Girls' Administration Building of the Newark City Home was a desolate and lonely place when this photo was taken. During cold winter days in the recent past, the gusting wind howled through broken windows creating an eerie and haunting environment. In 1993 the majority of the sanitarium buildings were demolished, ending an important era in area history.

Four
Striving to Move Faster

Since its early days, Verona has been constantly changing. The first major improvement in transportation came to Verona in 1806 when Israel Crane of Montclair organized a stock company that built the Newark and Pompton Turnpike—what we today know as Bloomfield and Pompton Avenues. Toll gates were established to finance interest on the stock and maintenance of the road. One of those gates was established at the top of the First Mountain in the area of Sunset Avenue. The new road provided a wider, improved, and more direct route for the early residents of the area. Not all, however, were pleased with the new road. Some resented the tolls, and, if possible, they would use "shunpikes" which bypassed the toll road. In 1871 Bloomfield Avenue became the first County-owned road in the state. This photo of Fillmore Condit was taken on Pompton Avenue about 1890.

An 1807 entry in an early sawmill ledger notes that loads of lumber were delivered to certain brooks for the turnpike company. This was undoubtedly used for the construction of bridges. This is the brownstone Bloomfield Avenue Bridge over the Peckman River as it appeared in a 1908 postcard. Its exact date of construction is unknown, but it is believed to have been built in the 1870s. This face of the bridge survives, but the opposite facade, on the Verona Lake side, was removed when the avenue was widened years ago.

For many years the only form of transportation through the area was by stage or, if personal fortune permitted, by the family carriage or wagon. Often people rode horseback or simply walked. The Youngs are seen in their family carriage on Elmwood Road in the 1890s preparing to embark on a Sunday outing (above), while the Ahlborns prepare to depart for church from the side of their elegant home on Fairview Avenue in the same period (below).

An attempt was made to improve transportation through Verona in the early 1870s when it was planned to build a railroad through the valley almost parallel to Bloomfield Avenue. Railroad gradings were created which survive to this day. The large earthen embankments shown in this c. 1908 postcard were constructed on each side of Verona Lake in preparation for a trestle. In 1872 work on a tunnel through the First Mountain was initiated and the Montclair entrance was still visible until recent years. The proposed rail line drew speculators to Verona, but the Panic of 1873 brought all work and dreams of fortune to an abrupt end.

The famed Olmsted firm was commissioned to redesign Verona Lake for Essex County in the early 1920s and had the island constructed between the large embankments on each shore. This was not only for aesthetic reasons, but to accommodate the railroad's right of way should the line ever be built. This postcard view dates to the early 1930s.

The railroad did come to Verona in 1890 but was built through the northern corner. A station was constructed at the head of Personette Street, but it was destroyed by fire in January 1905. Fortunately for Verona, construction on the new Caldwell station had just been completed, so the old station was brought to Verona. An old newspaper article records that the old Caldwell station was placed on runners and pulled by 12 horses down a snow-covered Bloomfield Avenue. These two photos were taken by Jon Glasby about 1940.

After the establishment of the railroad, new people came to Verona. A December 1892 news article noted that Verona had been partially aroused from its long and peaceful "Rip Van Winkle sleep." Originally the Bloomfield Avenue rail crossing was at grade, but for reasons of safety, the cut shown in this *c.* 1905 postcard was created and the railroad tunneled under Bloomfield Avenue. The underpass was eliminated in 1997.

The next major development in transportation to come to Verona was a trolley line on Bloomfield Avenue. In 1894 Verona Township passed an ordinance granting the North Jersey Street Railway Company the right to operate a street railway through the township. The trolley, however, was not considered an improvement by all, as opposition to its establishment was strong in Caldwell and Montclair. This photo was taken opposite Lakeside Avenue about 1912.

A news article noted that the opposition to the trolley in Caldwell consisted mainly of "the summer residents and carriage driving community which were decidedly in the minority." After several legal confrontations, the North Jersey Street Railway Company was given the approval to build their line, and in late summer of 1896 the two-lane track was ready for business. Opposition remained strong in Montclair, and it is said that the Montclair Town Council was controlled by the wealthy carriage-owning minority. The first trolleys traveled from Newark to the Montclair line and then from Verona to Caldwell. Hugh Mullen operated a stage, shown here about 1895, that transported trolley passengers and others through Montclair to Verona. Finally, in 1898, the Montclair Council capitulated and granted the trolley company the franchise; thus the gap was bridged and the area received a long delayed stimulus in growth.

The trolley did bring the hordes to Verona. The major attraction for many was Verona Lake, which became extremely popular in the early 1900s with the farmers' picnics in the summers and the skating matches in the winters. A spur led from the line on Bloomfield Avenue, providing partial access to Verona Lake. This Saunders Neck photo shows all the streetcars lined up on that spur about 1908.

Trolley service survived on Bloomfield Avenue until March 1952, when it finally gave way to buses. When the railroad tunnel under Bloomfield Avenue at Linn Drive was eliminated in 1997, the old trolley tracks were excavated, revealing the cobblestones and, beneath them, the old wooden ties that were remarkably well preserved. This 1940s photo was taken from the corner of Church Street looking west.

Following the improvements in transportation came new people who would build new homes. This mid-1890s photo shows Mr. Young standing alongside Elmwood Road. Mr. Young was an engraver who worked in New York and commuted to Verona. The two houses in the distance still stand but have been drastically changed. The building to the left is the former residence of Fillmore Condit.

New roads were established and large parcels which had served as farmland were divided into building lots. This postcard of the original clubhouse at the Montclair Golf Club shows Verona in the background. Barely noticeable is Hillcrest Terrace (seen to the left of the clubhouse roof). It was one of the new roads established around the turn of the century. As more people flocked to the area, lots were sold and new houses constructed.

Fairview Avenue was established in the 1890s and was considered one of Verona's most fashionable addresses. Large homes or estates were built like that of Henry Ahlborn, which still stands, and Glen Oaken—the home of Judge John L. Johnson, which was destroyed recently. These photos were taken about 1910 and show the first sidewalks under construction. The photo above was taken near Orchard Street looking north, while the photo below looks south from Linden Avenue.

The automobile was the mode of transportation that would bring about the greatest change not only in Verona, but also in other communities across the nation. It made out-of-the-way places accessible to the masses. Ava Williams is seated on the running board of her husband's 1912 Ford, which is parked in the driveway of 18 and 20 Otsego Road. The car was purchased for $375.

Five

Time to Recreate

When this photo was taken about 1908, Captain Hiram Cook was nearing the end of his long and useful life. During the Civil War, he had served as the captain of Company D, 5th New Jersey Volunteers. He came to Verona in the late 1860s to capitalize on the proposed rail line which never came to fruition. Cook purchased land between the area of present-day Wayland Drive and the east shore of Verona Lake. A major blow came in June 1869 when his first wife, Esther, died in childbirth. He later married Mary Jane Mills, who is seen in this photo.

Mary Jane was the daughter of John and Anna Mills. John and Anna, once known as Lord and Lady Mills, according to Irma Ott, were English immigrants. They settled in Verona on Sunset Avenue around the middle of the 19th century. This daguerreotype portrait of John was taken about 1850 and was rescued along with a photo of his wife, from a local house sale in 1986. The portrait of Mrs. Mills shows her holding what appears to be his photo.

Cook, a carpenter by trade, built and sold several homes on his property. About 1884 he built this Carpenter Gothic-style residence which overlooks Verona Lake where he and Mary Jane would spend the rest of their lives. Cook owned a good portion of the east shore of the lake, where people would frequently picnic without disturbing him or his family. According to family tradition, one day while Cook was sitting in his oak captain's chair on the front lawn, he got the idea to develop his lakefront property into a "Picnic and Pleasure Grounds." This photo was taken by Cook's son-in-law, Adolph Ott, about 1898.

Cook built a boathouse and bathhouse as well as a small pavilion where people were served refreshments. One of the highlights on the lake was Cook's small steam launch (Cook is shown here seated in the adjacent rowboat). The photographer to the right is said to have been Harry Trippett, who worked for *The Montclair Times*. This picture was taken about 1884.

Cook's venture fast became a favorite destination for churches, Sunday schools, and clubs throughout the area. He named the park "Eden Wild" after his daughter Floretta, whom he called Edie. She is seen in this *c.* 1884 photo seated in the rowboat. Lakeside Avenue is in the background.

These Young family photos were taken about 1896 and show Cook's boathouse and bathhouse. Cook's venture had a down side in that property owners on the west shore resented the noise and trespassing of picnickers on their properties. Consequently, the owner of the mill dam would occasionally draw down the water to a few inches of lakebottom prior to Cook's busy days. Then, his pavilion mysteriously burned. Despite the setbacks, the parkground survived and grew in popularity. Laurie Young is seated in the rowboat.

Captain Cook's son Ben enjoys a leisurely boat ride on Verona Lake about 1898. The large house in the background stood on the west corner of Lakeside Avenue and Pease and was known as the Barter Homestead.

Several families along Lakeside Avenue had their own private boathouses on the west shore of Verona Lake. To the left can be seen the ornate Victorian-era Cimiotti boathouse. The Cimiottis were among Verona's wealthiest families in the late 19th century.

Captain Cook was an ingenious man and in 1895 was granted a patent on his improved potato digger. It was his objective to create a tool that was less expensive to build, had increased efficiency, and avoided the use of gears that would be apt to clog when in use. Little is known about the success of his invention. This c. 1898 photo was taken to the rear of his house.

Cook was a family man and was considered stern but fair. This c. 1890 family portrait was taken on the back porch of the homestead, which still stands on Manor Road. Seated to the left is Ben, and to the right, his younger sister Cecelia. Standing behind Hiram and Mary Jane is Floretta and to the right is Edna. The captain had children by his first marriage who were young adults at this time.

Irma Ott, the only daughter of Floretta and Adolph, was born in the Cook Homestead in April 1900. She lived to the ripe age of 85 and enjoyed sharing her proud stories of the family and old Verona. Her grandmother is seen washing her moments after her birth.

Cook undoubtedly spent many hours at home contemplating the future of Eden Wild. In 1900 he decided to sell his portion of the lake frontage to the Verona Lake and Park Association, comprised of David Slayback, John Slayback, Charles Williams, and J.E. Williams. Cook and his wife died in 1911. Irma Ott recalled a small chest her grandmother had filled with family keepsakes. This was burned on the trash pile when the house was emptied.

The Verona Lake and Park Association, under the direction of Dave Slayback, made great changes including the construction of a new boathouse, a skatehouse, and a pavilion. Cook's old boathouse was removed. This c. 1905 postcard shows the railroad embankment to the left and the new boathouse to the right. Barely noticeable to the rear of the boathouse is the new pavilion. The old Cook Homestead can be seen to the upper right of the boathouse.

South of the new boathouse was this large merry-go-round, which may have dated to the Cook ownership. It was equipped with wooden horses and an organ all said to have been powered by a steam engine. The man standing on the step to the left is Charles Williams. Barely noticeable in the background to the right is Dave Slayback wearing a hat and bow tie. This postcard dates to 1905.

Among the new amusements added to Verona Lake was a small passenger steam train which operated on the east shore. This postcard view also dates to about 1905.

Of course Captain Cook's steam launch continued to be in service, and another launch was added which was named *Jean* after Dave Slayback's daughter. Taken about 1906, this postcard view shows Lakeside Avenue and the Barter Homestead in the background.

Commonly referred to as the skatehouse, this building was constructed adjacent to the dam and during the spring, summer, and fall, served as a boathouse. It originally had an open porch on the front, which had been enclosed by the time this photo was taken (*c.* 1912). Note the buildings on Bloomfield Avenue in the background.

About 1902 the dam was washed out and a new one constructed. Dave Slayback is seen holding a shovel in the center left of the picture. Note that he is not dressed in work clothes. Slayback was quickly becoming one of the most important citizens in Verona and would have a profound influence on the early development of the borough.

A formal picnic grove complete with tables was established adjacent to the boathouse and pavilion. It was a fine place to relax on a hot summer day. This postcard view dates to about 1907.

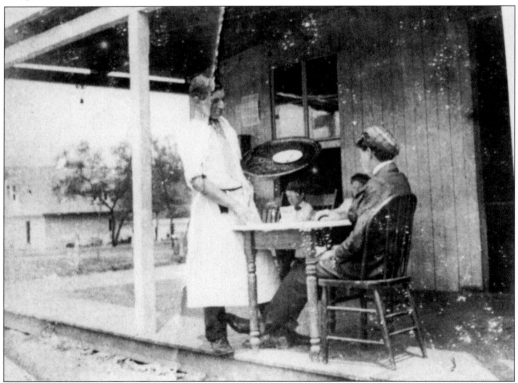

At the pavilion, patrons could purchase hamburgers and hot dogs, as well as a refreshing non-alcoholic beverage. Taken on July 10, 1903, this photo shows young Elmer Williams serving a customer.

It is perhaps hard to believe that at one time people actually swam in Verona Lake. An 1892 news story advised Verona's boys who were "not modest" to be discreet as "Bathing in the sunlight is not seemly." This postcard of discreet bathers dates to about 1905 and was taken north of the old boathouse. Swimming in the lake is believed to have been discontinued after several drownings.

Fun at Verona Lake was available to all—young and old, men and women. This c. 1906 postcard of "Arrivals" was taken on the walkway into the lake. The skatehouse is visible in the background.

Both rowboats and canoes were available for rental. Verona Lake became such a popular Mecca for pleasure seekers that postcards of it and the different activities available were printed by the thousands. Both of these views were taken about 1907. The one above shows the floodgates of the dam, and the one below shows the Cimiotti mansion (upper left corner), which once stood on Lakeside Avenue.

The major summer event at Verona Lake was the Grangers' Picnic, which was a combination of country fair and carnival. People flocked to the lake by the thousands. This photo shows parked carriages in the field north of the lake. The house in the background stood on the west side of Lakeview Place. It was eventually moved and today sits on the east side of Verona Place.

At the Grangers' Picnics were different activities and game booths that featured target shoots and ring toss—not much different from a carnival of today. The event usually ended with a fireworks display. Taken about 1907, this postcard shows the many booths with the pavilion in the background.

Saunders Neck took this photo of the Grangers' Picnic about 1908. One can't but notice the wonderful old cars. The automobile was becoming popular at this time. This picture is looking in the direction of the merry-go-round.

One of the most popular people to work at Verona Lake was the Swedish-born Pete Sinnirud, a speed skater. He is seen in this c. 1907 postcard standing on the dam by the floodgates. During the winter months, Pete was the center of attention. He was cheered by the crowds and feared by those who competed against him.

Pete Sinnirud was nicknamed the "Terrible Swede" because of his great speed. In 1901 Dave Slayback created the Verona Lake Skating Club in which Sinnirud was the star member. In 1904 he went to Christiana, Norway, and was a major success in the world championships. He is seen in this *c.* 1902 tin-type sporting the many medals he won.

Other amateur champions like Gil Bellefeuille (left) and Morris Wood performed on the lake, and the speed-skating meets for the United States amateur title were held there. The lake became a focal point for skating exhibitions, including barrel-jumping contests and skating on stilts. This *c.* 1907 postcard was taken at the north end of the lake looking east toward Bloomfield Avenue and Lakeview Place.

Old-time Verona residents remember the great fun that was had during the winter months. Children would race their friends, play games, or watch the adults. Both of these *c. 1907* postcards show the skatehouse. The upper view is in the direction of Lakeside Avenue where Our Lady of the Lake Church stands today.

Skating on Verona Lake, Verona, N. J.

Skating on Verona Lake was serious business in the early 1900s, and a sign containing a painted red ball hung on the front of the trolleys signifying that the ice on Verona Lake was safe and cleared of snow. Slayback served as president of the Eastern Skating Association and of the International Skating Union of America for a time. His influence helped to make Verona Lake a standard assignment for the daily newspapers. In 1920 the lake was acquired by Essex County.

Verona Lake was not the only recreation spot in the valley. The Montclair Golf Club moved to Verona in the 1890s and has been an important part of the community ever since. This turn-of-the-century postcard shows the original clubhouse which stood a short distance north of the present building. It was destroyed by fire in the 1920s.

The Verona Club was organized in 1894 for "social, intellectual, and recreative purposes." During their first year they built this clubhouse on the corner of Claremont and Derwent Avenues. It included a bowling alley and a billiard room which were located in the basement. The first service of the Congregational church was held here in 1896. The building still stands but has been extensively remodeled. This photo was taken about 1910.

In the early 1900s Charles Staedler purchased the building and operated a delicatessen and restaurant on a portion of the first floor. This wonderful interior photo was taken during World War I and shows Staedler's daughter, Thursa, behind the counter. He also ran the bowling alley and had two pool tables in the basement.

When chores were done, children found the time and opportunities to entertain themselves. The Young brothers are enjoying their spare time playing with a small boat beside their parents' home on Elmwood Road about 1896 (above), while the Harris brothers enjoy their homemade go-carts on Elmwood Road near the Young place about 1900 (below).

Adults also found time to break away from work and enjoy life. J.M. Harris is enjoying a bike ride on Claremont Avenue in front of his large home about 1898. In the background are the orchards on the Priest farm. This wonderful old photo was rescued from the trash.

Croquet was a favorite game of the 1890s and usually enjoyed on a Sunday or holiday. This 1898 photo was taken almost in the same location as the previous picture. From left to right are Al Harris; his cousin Malcolm; his father, J.M. Harris; his other cousin Marjorie; and his Uncle Will. Notice, in the distance, the Priest farmhouse and the white picket fence along Claremont Avenue.

Six

Sites of Lost Verona

It is unfortunate that with the passing of time, many of Verona's historic homes have fallen by the wayside and are now lost forever. An article in an 1892 edition of *The Caldwell News* noted that the destruction of a landmark was like a "blight upon life." It further states, "If there is a species of vandalism among our people, it shows itself in the disposition to demolish everything old, and substitute something new." This article was indeed ahead of its time. The loss of our heritage is a severe problem nationwide, and the preservation of historic sites is generally the exception than the rule. The Riker Homestead was among the first constructed in Verona and is identified on the Ashfield Map of 1787. In the late 1820s it became the home of Dr. Christian Bone and his wife. Bone came to America as a Hessian soldier during the Revolutionary War but changed sides shortly after his arrival. A celebrated herb doctor, he settled in Verona shortly after the war and for many years was the only doctor in the area. He died on Christmas morning, 1844, at the age of 101. This small dwelling was removed in the early 1920s to make way for the present-day middle school.

The Dobbins Homestead dated to the first quarter of the 19th century and was one of the oldest surviving dwellings in Verona in recent time. It stood on Bloomfield Avenue diagonally opposite the Verona Post Office and, prior to demolition, was the home of Stierles—a retail liquor store. This photo was taken in 1984.

Isaac Soverhill Dobbins (1787–1868) is believed to have built the Dobbins Homestead. According to family tradition, he conducted a charcoal business on his woodland properties in northern New Jersey. The Dobbins family were staunch supporters of the Verona Methodist Church. In 1833 the newly formed Board of Trustees of the church met in Isaac's home, where they resolved that each trustee would solicit for donations to build a new church.

Not long after the turn of the century, the old homestead was sold out of the Dobbins family. It was probably in the 1930s that the stores were built into the basement and first floor parlor area of the building. The small dining room and adjacent kitchen, along with small second-floor bedrooms, were used for storage. This photo was taken about 1940.

In March 1985, the Dobbins Homestead was demolished. During the removal, the old Victorian-era bay window was carefully removed along with many of the oak and pine hand-hewn timbers. The bay window has since been restored and remains in Verona in storage.

For many years small houses with eyebrow windows and side or rear kitchen wings were common in the area. This small residence stood on the east corner of Bloomfield Avenue and Church Street. It was built by Michael Kiefer, a carpenter, about 1852. This *c.* 1897 photo shows the steeple of the Congregational church in the background. Notice the old well adjacent to the side door and the important outhouse to the rear of the property. This house had been greatly remodeled in the first half of the 20th century. It was demolished in 1967 and replaced with a parking lot.

Michael and Anna Kiefer were born in Germany and immigrated to the United States in the 1830s. They moved to Verona with their growing family about 1850. During the Civil War, Michael enlisted into Company B of the 33rd Regiment, New Jersey Volunteers, which was also known as the 2nd Zouaves because of the style of their uniforms. He first saw action at the Battle of Chattanooga and participated in Sherman's March through Georgia. Kiefer was killed in August 1864 during the Siege of Atlanta. These two photos were taken in 1863 before Michael's Company broke camp in Newark.

Kiefer purchased his property from Daniel Williams, who lived in a house next door that was also built in the early 1850s (to the west on the opposite side of Church Street). The 1860 Federal Census reveals that Daniel and his wife were raising seven children in this house. His father, Zadock, also resided with them. This watercolor was painted in 1891. The Verona Rescue Squad stands in the approximate location of the barn.

Next to the Daniel Williams place, where Home Liquors is today, stood the home of Zadock and Mary Williams, which was built in the mid-1850s. This house was perched high on a bank overlooking Bloomfield Avenue. The property descended to Mr. and Mrs. Hiram Handville. Hiram served as one of the first law enforcement officers of Verona. The house was demolished in 1967.

Farther west on the north side of Bloomfield Avenue stood the Thomas Ettenborough Homestead, which dated to the middle of the 19th century. The prosperous Ettenboroughs ran the nearby gristmill at Verona Lake. This photo was taken about 1940. Today Richfield Caterers stands on the site.

The Haight House stood on Bloomfield Avenue where present-day Terry's Drugs is located. It was a small building constructed in the mid-19th century with a few mid-Victorian-era embellishments, including the small porch and front gable with arched windows. The young girl in front of the house is Vesta Bowden, and she is pictured with her dog Prince. The picture was taken about 1915.

Until recently, the Davenport Homestead stood on Bloomfield Avenue at the corner of Linn Drive. The property was purchased by Archibald and Henrietta Davenport in 1859, and it is believed that the original portion of the building was standing at that time. Archibald established a blacksmith shop west of the house in 1860, and his son, George W., took over the business in 1881 and ran it until his retirement in 1908. When the Civil War broke out, George enlisted for service, but his father, feeling that he was too young for combat, brought him home. He was more successful when he again enlisted in 1863. George operated a small farm adjacent to the house. He grew corn and had an apple and peach orchard. Cows grazed near the railroad tracks. A large barn and a small springhouse were located behind the house. Verona's new community center now occupies this site.

The William Baldwin Homestead stood on the west side of Pompton Avenue between Bloomfield and Claremont Avenues. Thought to date to the 1840s, it passed to William's son Bill, who for years worked in Marley's quarry across the road. Prior to demolition in the 1940s, Walter Williams discovered an early ice skate and a stack of early local newspapers. One wonders what fascinating relics were left behind. This photo dates to about 1908.

Southwest of the Baldwin House, on the corner of Bloomfield and Pompton Avenues, stood this building, which is identified as the shoe shop of William Baldwin on an 1874 map. Little is known about the origin of this structure other than it can be traced as far back as 1850. The White Castle later occupied this site. This picture was located in the collection of the Newark Library and is believed to date to about 1918.

Dewitt C. Baldwin's house stood on the south side of Sunset Avenue east of Mount Prospect. This beautiful Victorian-style farmhouse was one of the finest and most well kept in Verona. It was probably built in the 1860s on property that originally belonged to Dewitt's father, Lucas. On the farm Dewitt grew corn, wheat, and oats and also had apple and peach orchards. Baldwin's grandson recalled that Dewitt developed and produced a type of western corn which became known around New Jersey as Baldwin sweet white corn. Baldwin was well respected in the community and was a staunch supporter of the Methodist Church. His father reputedly built the house next door which still stands and will be pictured in the next chapter. As for Dewitt's house, it has long passed into history and a new home now stands on the site. This exquisite photo dates to about 1890.

The J.E. DeCamp House stood on the south side of Bloomfield Avenue east of Verona Place and probably was built in the 1880s. DeCamp was a butcher, and in the old barn behind the house were discovered two sets of racks with hand-forged meat hooks. The house and barn were demolished in the 1970s, and a condominium complex now stands on this site.

Remembered as the Maron House, this building dated to about the same period as the DeCamp House. It stood on the south side of Bloomfield Avenue west of Brookdale, where the building occupied by Hoffman Floors stands today. An 1890s map reveals that it was once owned by Anson A. Voorhees. When this picture was taken in the 1920s, the original clapboard siding had been covered with stucco.

Verona contained a diverse mixture of people who settled in the valley for different reasons. The seafaring Captain William Pease brought his family to Verona in 1847 with the hope of preventing his sons from following in his footsteps. His son, John, was enticed to the sea. Many old-timers remember this as the Barter Homestead—William's daughter, Emma Jane, married Albion Barter. The house was being razed when this photo was taken about 1930.

By the 1920s the Cimiotti House, which overlooked Verona Lake from the west side of Lakeside Avenue, had become the fashionable "Dincins' Lakeside Terrace" restaurant. The mansion was built around 1881, and Captain Cook served as the architect and contractor. The Cimiottis made their money in furs as did the Hornfecks, who resided in a large house next door. A modern housing development now occupies this site.

Built in the 1890s, the Carl Mau House stood a short distance southwest of the Cimiotti House. To the rear of the home was a carriage house and windmill. This elegant mansion has been replaced with a modern housing development. Dating to the late 1890s, this photo was reproduced from a glass slide—one of only two known to exist of Verona.

Glen Oaken was built in the 1890s in the Queen Anne Victorian style and occupied the west corner of Fairview Avenue and Personette Street. Originally the home of Judge John L. Johnson, it is more recently remembered as the Wilder home. A beautiful stained-glass window adjacent to the front doorway included the name of the estate within its patterns. Tragically, this historic home was recently replaced by a modern dwelling.

Dr. Henry B. Whitehorne was one of the most admired people in old Verona. After studying medicine at the Albany Medical College, he moved to Verona around 1874 to assist Dr. Personett. His Grove Avenue home was built in the early 1890s and stood opposite Reid Place. Unfortunately, it was razed years ago, and the site is now an overgrown vacant lot. At the age of 18, Whitehorne enlisted in the navy and served on the gunboat *Wyalusing* as captain's clerk and signal officer. After Lee's surrender, he rejoined the navy and served much of his time abroad. He left navy life in 1870. Dr. Whitehorne was a kind and gentle man who was always available to help anyone in the community in their time of need. In recognition of his tireless devotion to Verona, in 1928 the new high school, now the middle school, was named in his honor. He was also a founder of Mountainside Hospital.

Seven
The Survivors

Although Verona has lost a good portion of its historic homes, some survive and serve as reminders that the present is a product of the past. The home thought to be the oldest standing is the Enos Martin Homestead, located on the north corner of Martin Road and Beach Street. The smaller block of the house was built prior to 1787 and contains a large hearth along with the remains of a beehive bake oven. Overhead ceiling beams in the first-floor keeping room were finished with an adz and meant to be exposed. The large block of the house was built in the 1830s during the Greek Revival era. Enos Martin was a prominent figure in early Verona. He served the Patriot cause during the Revolutionary War and was a justice of the peace for many years. The house remained in his family for over a century. Currently, it is being restored.

The Priest farmhouse is located at 110 Claremont Avenue and was probably constructed in the first quarter of the 19th century. The original keeping room is located in the basement and features a large cooking hearth with swinging crane. Reverend Priest purchased the farm in 1873 perhaps for speculation and for his upcoming retirement. Under his direction the original house was remodeled and expanded into the mid-Victorian style. He was a Presbyterian pastor and served in that capacity in Montclair from 1858 to 1861. He purchased the farmhouse while serving in Quincy, Illinois. The home later became the residence of Al Harris and his family. Al is seen standing on the porch roof in this *c.* 1940 photo.

On the opposite side of Claremont Avenue east of the Priest farmhouse stands the Ougheltree Homestead. Its date of construction remains a mystery; however, the Ashfield Map of 1787 labels a dwelling on this site. It is possible that a portion of the building dates to this time or perhaps it replaced the original dwelling. Prior to being remodeled, the house displayed many Victorian-era details as shown in this *c.* 1940 photo.

The finest unspoiled early-19th-century farmhouse in Verona is located at 190 Grove Avenue. Its date of construction and the name of its original owner are unknown. John Brower lived here with his family during the second half of the 19th century. The smaller wing contains a large hearth. Some of the exterior walls are brick lined—a technique called nogging. This was an early form of insulation.

The I.C. Shafer Homestead is located on the south corner of Sunset Avenue and Glen Road. The original portion is believed to date to the early 1800s, and an 1850 map identifies it as the residence of William Corby. The house was expanded and remodeled during the Shafer ownership in the mid-Victorian era. It contains a beautiful banister with newel posts and spindles of walnut and an ornate plaster cornice in the formal parlor.

West of the Shafer place is this home once owned by Dewitt Baldwin (his residence is shown in the previous chapter and stood next door). This house would appear to date to the late Victorian era; however, it is reported that a portion of it dates back beyond this vintage. This may have been the home of Lucas Baldwin, Dewitt's father. The house looks much the same today as it did in 1904.

Lucas Baldwin (1802–1872) was a staunch Methodist, and in the winter of 1831–32, the first Methodist meetings were held in his home. He and his wife raised 11 children. This ambrotype portrait photo was taken about 1860.

On the north side of Sunset Avenue west of Mount Prospect stands the Marshall Baldwin Homestead. Marshall is best remembered for a home remedy handed down in the family—said to cure skin cancers and growths. Some handwritten documents that date to the 1830s verify that the cure worked. Unfortunately, its ingredients are lost. Built prior to 1850, the Baldwin House was added and extended late in the Victorian era.

The Gould Mansion was a show place owned by a prominent family. It stands on the west side of Rockland Terrace and faces Bloomfield Avenue. The front and back parlors contain high-style Greek Revival mantels, and a large staircase wraps around from the first floor to the attic. In the basement are two hearths, both of which are equipped with the remains of beehive ovens. The house would appear to date from the 1830s.

North of Bloomfield Avenue on the west side of Grove stands the former residence of Dr. Stephen Personett. The date of the original portion of this house is uncertain but it appears on an 1850 map. Surviving interior features include a mid-Victorian-era staircase and a decorative plaster cornice in the parlor. Stephen's great-grandfather is believed to have settled in Verona in 1740 on land northeast of this property.

Stephen Personett was born in 1813. Early in life he took an interest in medicine and began as a clerk in a Newark drugstore. In June 1834, he was granted a medical diploma by the Medical Society of New Jersey. At some date prior to 1850 he opened a drugstore on the north corner of Grove and Bloomfield Avenues. The doctor also served as a local justice of the peace for a time, and connected with the store was his office where legal business was transacted. In 1847–48 he served as a representative in the New Jersey State Legislature. His long and useful life came to an end in February 1880 as the result of a carriage accident that occurred while on his return home from a party at Dewitt Baldwin's. Like Dr. Whitehorne, Dr. Personett was a man loved by all in the community.

The Isaac N. Dobbins House originally stood on Bloomfield Avenue at the corner of South Prospect. Built in the mid-19th century, the house features a Greek Revival–era front doorway with sidelights and a transom. Years ago the building was removed from its original site and moved around the corner to South Prospect Street, where it stands today. The old wagonhouse stood to the rear of the house and was recently demolished.

This portrait photo of the Dobbins family was taken about 1875. Seated from left to right are Catharine Hedden Dobbins, daughter Bertha, son Justus Dobbins, and Isaac N. Dobbins. Justus would later move into his grandfather's house and reside there with his family until moving to Freehold in 1910.

On the point of Claremont and Bloomfield Avenues near Verona Center was built this small residence which was originally occupied by Zabina Williams and family. It was built about 1863 and today serves as the Verona Barber Shop. Zabina had three children—George W., who served during the Civil War; Cornelius, who occupied a house on Claremont Avenue; and Charles, who died in 1864 at the age of 22. This picture, taken about 1940, shows the building in its original state.

George Williams and his wife, Pauline, would eventually occupy the old home on Bloomfield Avenue, and it would remain in the family until after the turn of the century. George enlisted in 1864 as a private in Company H, 39th Regiment of the New Jersey Volunteer Infantry, and was honorably discharged the following year. He re-enlisted into Company I, 9th Regiment U.S. Regular Infantry, and was on duty on the Western frontier and had frequent engagements with hostile tribes. He was honorably discharged at Sidney Barracks in Nebraska. His profession after military service was that of a carpenter. While building the Parkhurst House on Bloomfield Avenue in 1888, he suffered a tragic fall which resulted in his having to be hospitalized for many years. He died in 1896 and was buried at the old burial ground in Cedar Grove. When this tin-type photo was taken about 1880, George was about 35 years old.

The Brady Homestead stands on the north side of Bloomfield adjacent to Henry's and was built about 1869, after the marriage of Michael Brady to Elizabeth Kiefer. Family members recall that the first-floor parlor was only used for weddings and funerals. In the parlor hung an engraving of the notorious Libby Prison, where Michael was held captive by the Confederates during the Civil War. This photo dates to about 1930.

The portrait of Michael Brady was taken about 1880. Brady served in Company D, 5th New Jersey Volunteers. In 1862 he was shot in the ankle, and following the Gettysburg conflict, he was taken prisoner. Held in captivity for about six and a half months, he was eventually released in a prisoner exchange. He rejoined his regiment and served until the expiration of his term.

Built after the Civil War, the Cornelius Williams Homestead stands on Claremont Avenue diagonally opposite Church Street. Tradition holds that the wood used in building the house came from California and was shipped around South America and up the East Coast. Walter Williams Sr., who resided here, recalled the Blizzard of '88 and how snow had drifted to the second-floor windows. The house has undergone changes since this *c.* 1940 photo was taken.

On the east side of the Williams House stands the Burd House, which probably dates to the 1880s. The house has undergone much remodeling since this photo was taken about 1940, but it still contains its narrow stairway to the second floor.

Across Claremont Avenue from the Cornelius Williams House stands the former home of Jennie Parker. Built in the mid-1890s in the Queen Anne Victorian style, it was beautifully refurbished by its current owners, Mr. and Mrs. Ballerini. It contains a period staircase with newel post, spindles, and handrails of chestnut. The residence on the adjacent lot once served as the carriage house.

To the rear of the present-day International House of Pancakes on Bloomfield Avenue stands this house believed to have been the residence of John Simonson, who operated the adjacent blacksmith shop. Probably built about 1870, the house retains its original Victorian-era staircase among other period features.

Captain Cook built this ornate mansard-roofed, Victorian-era home on the corner of Sunset Avenue and Mountain View Road in the early 1870s. Prior to building his Carpenter Gothic-style home which overlooks Verona Lake, he and his family resided here. When this photo was taken in February 1901, the house had seen little change from when it was built.

One of the finest examples of mid-Victorian architecture is the Johnson Home, which stands on the west side of Grove Avenue behind Center Drugs. Dating to the 1880s, the house, until recently, contained its original decorative slate roof shown in this 1984 photo.

Little information has been uncovered to date on this home, which stands on the south side of Brookdale Avenue. A twin dwelling stood next door where Celentano's parking lot is today. Both buildings were built in the 1880s. The former dwelling was the residence of a Mrs. King, whose sister, Anna DeGolier, founded the Isabella Literary Club. The first library of the club was housed in that dwelling.

The Stephen Walker House, built in the 1890s and seen here about 1910, is located on Bloomfield Avenue opposite the Verona Post Office. Dr. Archer Bush is seated in his Hupmobile. He practiced medicine in Verona from about 1907 to 1918, when he was called to active duty in the army. He married Helen Dobbins in 1921.

Many families moved to Verona in the 1890s as the village slowly transformed into a bedroom community. Fillmore Condit had Overlook Cottage built in the 1890s on the east side of Elmwood Road above his home on Bloomfield Avenue. It overlooks Everett Field, which he donated to the borough in 1910 and was later named in memory of his son. This photo was taken about 1895 when the R.J. Young family resided there.

Built about 1896 in a field of wild flowers, the Youngs' new home stood on the west side of Elmwood Road. This is one of the most fascinating photos of old Verona because it provides a rare opportunity of seeing a building under construction. Elmwood Road terminated at Claremont Avenue where a cottage stood on the opposite side owned by Dr. Priest. The house at the far right was the Harris residence on Claremont Avenue.

The Youngs moved into their new home in the closing years of the 19th century. The old tower section of the house was removed for some unknown reason about 50 years ago.

The Youngs were among Verona's well-to-do families. These interior photos (right and p. 124) were taken about 1899 and show some of the rooms as they were originally furnished and wallpapered. All woodwork was naturally finished. Note the kerosene lamp next to the piano in the one photo and a smaller lamp on the table next to Mrs. Young in the other. Also note the popcorn chain on the lower portion of the Christmas tree. The Barnum circus poster and other toys under the tree were for the Youngs' two boys and would today be worth a small fortune.

John M. Harris, a New York businessman, moved to Verona with his family in 1893 and built this large home on the south side of Claremont Avenue east of Elmwood Road. The family is pictured on the front lawn. The old kerosene post lamp in the foreground survives and is presently kept in storage. The Harris House was five years old when this photo was taken.

Before the end of the century Harris had two additional homes constructed on his property for speculation. This home was built next to his in 1898. Work on the house was in the process of completion when this photo was taken. Notice the scaffold suspended from hooks anchored to the boxline gutter. The homes in the background stood on Bloomfield Avenue.

The 1890s were indeed a time of expansion for the sleepy little hamlet of Verona. Charlie Simonson built his large home on the west corner of Bloomfield Avenue and South Prospect Street. From his front door he could keep a watchful eye on his store across the avenue and a short distance to the east. In later years his home was moved around the corner and an automotive business now occupies the original site.

About the time of his retirement from seafaring life in 1899, Captain John Pease had his home built on the north corner of Lakeside and Pease Avenues. Among its original occupants were three parrots that were well versed in the English language. The Pease property originally stretched down to the west shore of Verona Lake.

A short distance north and adjacent to the rectory of Our Lady of the Lake stands the Charles Bahr Homestead, built in the 1890s. Bahr, a German immigrant, came to Verona in the 1870s. Only a month before his death in 1923, he and his son founded the lumber company on Durrell Street. This photo was taken about 1913, and the old house, to this day, remains in the Bahr family.

It was not uncommon for an old house to be moved years ago—an early form of recycling. According to the late William Graham, the house on the east corner of Grove and Linden Avenues once served as the print shop of the Newark City Home prior to removal to its present site. It became the home of the widow Christine Dollmaier, who remodeled and updated it in the late Victorian style in the early 1900s.

No photographic history of Verona would be complete without including the elegant Kip's Castle. Built on the ridge of the First Mountain at the turn of the century, the stone mansion features breathtaking views of points east and west. Its woodwork is no less breathtaking with rooms of paneled oak and other fine woods. A small chapel room with cathedral ceiling and mahogany mantelpiece is located on the first floor. Frederick Kip was successful in the textile industry. Stone walls surround his estate, creating a European baronial atmosphere. For nearly a century Kip's Castle, like a sentinel, has stood watch over Verona (and points east) and has witnessed its change from a rural community to a suburban one. If only its walls could talk, they would tell of the many buildings they have seen rise and fall in the valley to the west. But like the other landmarks that survive, it tells the story of a bygone era and gives its own history lesson. Collectively, our historic sites remind us that we can't know where we are going until we know and understand where we have been.